HOW TO START A FOUNDATION

Quinn Chapman

TLM Publishing House

Social Stamina – 1,2,3 Let's Go!

Titles to help look at things from other perspectives and strengthen your mindset.

The Great Ascension–1,2,3 Let's Go!

Titles to help you gain focus and climb the ladder of success!

How to Start – 1,2,3 Let's Go!

Titles to help you with step-by-step, must-have knowledge of the business world and personal experiences.

Top 10 Questions to Ask Before You…1,2,3 Let's Go!

Titles with must-have questions (and logic behind) for many of life's daily and major decisions.

Find our fiction below!

https://www.ttpublishinghouse.com/legendsreborn

https://www.ttpublishinghouse.com/7wishes

https://www.ttpublishinghouse.com/mallcadet

Social Media

Facebook: tlmpublishinghouse

Website: www.TTpublishinghouse.com

Want to Read for Free?

You may qualify for a spot on our Advance Reader Copy group.

Never heard of an ARC Group?

Simply put, it's a small group of people who are interested in a specific genre and are invited to read books before they're published.

Your feedback can help alter the storyline or even catch an elusive typo!

You're asked to provide an honest review when it is published, and that's it!

You read for free!

Go now to confirm your interest in the ARC Group!
https://www.ttpublishinghouse.com/joinTLMarc

Get Your Free Gift!

Business needs consistency, consistency needs a plan. With this free planner, you'll have a planner that you can print and hang on your wall to keep your life consistent for yourself and everyone around you. Use it for your company or your personal well-being,

Grab the year-wide planner below!

Go now to https://www.dontstopuntil.com/30d-ss-getyourplanner **(Yes! It's totally FREE!)**

Contents

Start with Performance Planning

The Difference Between a Private Foundation and a Public Charity

The Internal Revenue Service (IRS) has **approved** the formation of tax-exempt nonprofit organizations. There are either private foundations or public charities among these organizations. A single donor, often an individual or a corporation, endows a private foundation with money to create it.

Using funds obtained from the general populace, a public charity actively promotes its operations. The method of securing financing is the most significant distinction between the two.

To be eligible for tax-exempt charitable status, both must exist for a charitable purpose, for example, to help people or animals. A private foundation is a charity created by a single donor, who is often a person or a business. The word "public charity" refers to the frequent solicitation of communal contributions. The most important distinction between a private foundation and a public charity is the method of fund-raising. A private foundation is often supported by a single source endowment, while a public charity must regularly request contributions from individuals and organizations.

A private foundation may make donations to a public charity, but not vice versa. In general, public charities have higher gift restrictions than private foundations. Individuals are attracted to giving to public charities due to the freedom they have while doing so. Thus, tax tactics may be adjusted to individual preferences.

Define your Purpose

There are several reasons why individuals opt to establish nonprofit organizations. Some individuals are naturally motivated to assist others. Many individuals who have been directly touched by a social affliction—sickness, disease, natural catastrophe, or lack of access to basic needs and resources—aspire to contribute to its treatment. Others may want to raise funds for a worthy cause.

Regardless of your motive, outlining your aim in detail, including your goals and activities, is the most crucial step in influencing your cause effectively. If your 501(c)(3) tax exemption application lacks a clearly stated objective, the IRS may deny it. Starting a business without a nonprofit and long-term success strategy is risky.

Write a Mission Statement for your Foundation

Ask yourself the following questions while deciding the purpose of your business: Who, What, Where, When, Why, and How? Why are you establishing a charitable organization?

What is the function of your business? What are you attempting to rectify? What ideals will guide the actions of your organization?

Who will be your organization's intended audience or beneficiaries? Who will be in control of the services and resources of your organization? Who are the key influencers who will assist your organization in getting support? Who are the prospective members of your board of directors and staff?

How will you achieve your objective? What initiatives will you oversee, and how will funds be distributed? How will you pay for the management of programs and services? How will the procedures be funded?

Where will your task be completed? Is this a municipal, state, or regional initiative, or a national or international one?

After answering these questions, you may begin developing a three-year action plan for your organization, complete with planned activity milestones, impact targets, budget estimates, and other specifics.

Choose Between a Nonprofit and a Trust

When creating a private foundation, donors must choose between a nonprofit company and a trust. The choice will have long-term consequences. To assist you in considering crucial aspects, we've compiled a collection of typical questions and answers.

One of the first considerations you'll have to make when founding a private foundation is whether to organize it as a nonprofit company or a trust. Because the kind of company you choose will have long-term ramifications, it's vital to think about all of the difficulties early on.

Compile frequently asked questions and answers, outlining the most important things to consider while forming a private foundation.

Both types of organizations need a governing document. A certificate of incorporation must be submitted to the secretary of state to establish a company. The state in which the nonprofit was formed should also be examined; since certain jurisdictions have more advantageous rules and regulations for nonprofits. Bylaws that give more precise operational requirements must be created by the nonprofit organization.

The need to register a trust varies per state since the legal jurisdiction is defined by the grantor's nexus. Whether a nonprofit is a corporation or a trust, its bylaws should contain language emphasizing its charitable mission and mentioning Internal Revenue Code Section 508 (e), which limits operations to exempt purposes.

A private foundation formed as a corporation is more flexible than a trust since the board of directors has complete power. The board of directors has the power to amend the bylaws, the corporation's domicile, and even the benevolent aim of the foundation. Flexibility is important to many families because it enables the foundation to expand and adapt to changing community needs as well as changing family opinions across generations. If the founders are concerned about mission drift, they may make tiny donations to limit the foundation's humanitarian purposes.

A trust is less adaptable than a private foundation organized as a corporation. Private foundations established as trusts have more constraints than nonprofit corporations. Making alterations to a trust needs court permission to change the governing agreement as well as the participation of the attorney general in many countries. Permission is allowed for a court to amend a foundation's benevolent purpose, but only if it can be shown that the charity goal is difficult to carry out or illegal—a high hurdle to cross. A trust arrangement protects founders who are worried about future generations "hijacking" their firm and goals.

There are no longer any limits on for-profit and nonprofit enterprises operating. Nonetheless, trust perpetuity is prohibited in certain jurisdictions. In most cases, any entity type will serve the founders' and successors' temporal scope in perpetuity.

It is necessary to assess the corporate types of foundations that recognize unrelated business income tax (UBIT). Trusts pay a higher tax rate than businesses on average. When a foundation engages in a transaction or activity that is unrelated to its tax-exempt purpose, the UBIT is triggered. When a founder's estate plan includes leaving the company's assets to a foundation, this is common.

It's crucial to look at the entity types of foundations that recognize unrelated company income tax. Foundations should examine debt-financed income, which is subject to UBIT and may derive from investments in certain partnerships and LLCs.

Private foundations, whether organized as a nonprofit corporation or a trust, must pay a 1.39 percent excise tax on investment income, which includes interest, dividends, and capital gains. Directors and officials of non-profit companies are not liable for corporate debts. When it comes to making business judgments, trustees are held to a higher standard than companies. Officers, directors, and trustees are able to delegate investment management and foundation administration to professional advisers. Furthermore, director, trustee, and officer insurance are offered to give further liability protection, regardless of the firm's structure.

Which one is better is up for debate. Each foundation is unique, and it may be founded and run according to the founders' wishes. It is vital to understand the aims and objectives of a private foundation before founding and maintaining it. The trade-off between flexibility and control, as well as who is willing and competent to run the foundation, is often debated when it comes to succession planning. People should additionally consider the following items:

- Investing and funding considerations: What resources will you employ to fund your foundation, and what will your contributions entail?

- Management and organization – How much power and engagement do you want now and in the future? Who else will be participating, if anybody, and what will they contribute?

We often discover that people have not considered all parts of the process and need more time. Rushing through the procedure leads to poor outcomes and money lost that cannot be recovered. Working with a group of experts, such as an experienced attorney, a CPA, and an investment adviser; enhances the likelihood of creating the correct firm the first time. Investing time **upfront** will result in more conviction and happiness in the long term.

Register your Foundation with the IRS

Request a taxpayer identification number (EIN). Obtain Form SS-4PDF in order to apply for an employment identification number. You may submit an EIN application online, via mail, or by fax. If your organization was created outside the U.S. or U.S. territories, you may also apply by phone.

Apply for tax exemption with the IRS. To get 501(c)(3) status (or the equivalent in your country) and allow tax-deductible contributions, you will need the assistance of competent specialists, but it is a necessary step. If these professionals contribute their time or participate on your board, the foundation may save a substantial amount of money. In many situations, however, it is advantageous to use specialists who can make all the difference.

File for exemption from taxation with your state. The next step is to provide the IRS with organizational documents. In addition, applicants are required to pay a fee. It must be completed and filed electronically via the IRS website.

File a tax exemption claim with your state. Upon IRS approval of your tax-exempt status, submit any further paperwork required to get tax-exempt status from your state.

Advantages of Establishing a Private Foundation

Giving via a private foundation provides many benefits over donating as an individual. Several examples follow. Individuals and families get large tax advantages from private foundations. Individual donors often file their tax deductions in a hurry at the end of the year, but private foundations may afford you the possibility of taking a more measured approach. You gain the tax benefit by establishing a private foundation and then making your philanthropic contributions gradually over time. Despite the fact that donations to your foundation are irreversible and must be utilized for philanthropic purposes, you and your family have discretion over how these funds are spent and disbursed.

You can give appreciated assets to your foundation, such as long-held low-basis shares, and get a tax deduction for the full fair market value with a five-year carryforward of up to 30% of your AGI. Most foundations are constructed to last forever. In contrast to a direct donation, which benefits a single recipient on a certain occasion, a foundation extends your family's generosity and enhances your **reputation beyond** your lifetime. Individuals may just send a check, whereas private foundations need board approval for financing.

Even if your foundation's board consists of just direct family members, you will be able to reject undesired financial aid requests without feeling guilty. A private foundation enables you to give direct aid to people and families while conserving money. Private foundations may send gifts directly to foreign charitable organizations, even if there is no 501 (c) (3) intermediary authorized by the IRS, and they may run scholarship programs and choose applicants with prior IRS approval. In addition to contributing cash to others, a private foundation may conduct its activities.

Consider providing a nonprofit organization (such as a charter school or church) with a low-interest loan instead of a grant to begin building a new facility while conducting a capital campaign. If you operate a private foundation, all legitimate and reasonable expenses incurred in pursuit of the foundation's philanthropic aims count toward your minimum distribution obligation. If you establish a foundation, you may pay competent people for their foundation-related work, even if the foundation is managed by family members.

Advantages of Establishing a Nonprofit Organization

Nonprofit organizations with a social mission include public charities, foundations, churches, fraternal organizations, and chambers of commerce. They include a vast array of organizations, including non-governmental ones (NGOs).

Nongovernmental organizations are often concerned with global issues. In order to qualify for the 501(c) federal corporation income tax exemption, organizations with a charitable mission must be excluded from paying taxes. Upon adoption of this exemption, the majority of charitable organizations are free from state and local taxes.

This viewpoint also enhances the likelihood of charitable contributions, since people are more likely to give to organizations that help them reduce their tax liability. A gift or donation made to a 501(c)(3) organization is tax-deductible. Additionally, nonprofit organizations may seek funding from private and public sources.

Once a nonprofit is founded, the founders are fully separated from the organization. Consequently, individual founders are no longer accountable for debts, lawsuits, penalties, and other legal concerns.

Employees and directors of a nonprofit organization have limited liability. The private assets of a nonprofit's founders are hidden from creditors and courts. If a person behaves unlawfully or unethically while hiding behind the charity's shield, they will be held liable if the charity suffers injury.

The nonprofit organization has legal standing and an identity apart from its founders. This feature may appeal to anybody desiring to establish a mission-driven organization with a long lifespan. Donors are more likely to contribute to organizations that they feel will have a lasting impact.

How to Keep your Private Foundation Running

Trustees of a foundation may be paid for their activities. If they obey the regulations, certainly. Should they be reimbursed, however? The answers to the provoking question are opposites. The more vociferous and fervent side of the discussion is opposed to the other side.

Our answer is measured: if properly administered, reasonable compensation for trustees may be justified and withstand public and IRS scrutiny. However, if your foundation pays or is considering paying trustee fees, the following should be considered.

One-fourth of American foundations pay trustees. A quarter of all foundations in the United States provide salaries, fees, or stipends to their trustees. The amount of compensation depends on the size and kind of the foundation, as well as the mode of board service.

Trustees of private foundations may be rewarded in three ways under the current regulations. They may be compensated for professional services such as accounting, legal, investment, and banking, as well as for grantmaking as a program officer or executive director. They may be compensated for "regular" service. This is equivalent to an annual or per-meeting stipend or modest remuneration for board work.

Appropriate compensation is permitted provided trustees stick to certain service areas and refrain from self-dealing. Self-dealing by the management, directors, or family members of private foundations is a different subject.

Objections concerning the compensation of trustees:

When disputes happen averse to trustee compensation, it is usually identified among these categories: ethical or trustees should not be remunerated for charity work, reformist or abuses must be given attention, or good governance or the limits between the board and staff must be maintained.

According to the ethical argument, private foundations have no incentive to reward board members since public charities do so rarely. The IRS classifies private foundations as 501(c)(3) charitable organizations, similar to public charities.

The rationale for the change is a few instances of trustee misconduct. Several board members have received grossly inflated salaries or none at all for their work on behalf of the organization. Even though the law mandates that trustee compensation be fair and reasonable, enforcement and liability remain the exception.

Although these two points get the most attention, the question of good governance may be more significant. The nonprofit sector is most successful when there is a clear distinction between decision-making (often a board seat) and execution (usually a professional service function).

Given that the majority of foundation boards are small, collegial, and may include family members, blurring this barrier may impair board judgment and cause chaos during periods of poor performance.

Justification for trustee compensation:

Trustees' salaries are rarely considered in the context of total staff and board salaries, which are a subset of foundation administration costs. These overall costs, which include grantmaking, accounting, investment, and legal, *may be* pricey for unpaid foundation trustees.

Effective grantmaking requires enough time. Given that the majority of foundations are tiny and lack professional employees, it is fair to depend on and compensate trustees to carry out staff responsibilities. If a trustee's primary duty is grantmaking, he or she cannot be distinguished from a paid employee.

Compensation may be required to entice busy professionals or highly regarded people who would experience financial hardship if they served on a board for free.

Foundations that compensate trustees must adhere to these criteria. As with so many other aspects of foundation administration, trustee salaries are a matter of personal preference. Here are some guidelines for foundations with paid trustees:

Resolve the moral dilemma. Some boards will provide compensation to trustees, while others will not. The trustees must first participate in an open debate and develop an agreement on this issue. After a board has established its compensation philosophy and developed a pay system, it is crucial that the highest ethical standards are adhered to.

It is essential to provide fair pay in addition to basic compensation for routine services. Paid trustees must at the very least account for their time and justify their salary in terms of billable hours, notwithstanding the complexity of the issue of fairness. It is also essential to maintain administrative expenditures in proportion to charitable donations; a foundation that provides $100,000 must justify administrative costs of $100,000.

Govern with prudence. If trustees are highly rewarded for professional, as opposed to everyday, duties, there should be a way to evaluate their performance. Theoretically, a highly paid trustee should be subject to a yearly evaluation. This strategy doesn't have to be hard to understand, but it may need a specific tool, like an outside review or a special board committee.

Leadership with honor:

A board of directors should keep in mind that private foundations are not private and should behave as though they are being observed. Few foundations pay their trustees, and many in business believe this practice should be eliminated. On the website www.GuideStar.org, all nonprofit organizations, including private foundations, may access salary information. This openness serves as a reminder that all grantmaking, regardless of its level of personalization, belongs in the public sphere.

Fundraising

Set up a Donor Advised Fund

Donor-advised funds might help your private foundation. These giving vehicles provide the advantages of a private foundation without the administrative load, including the option to tailor your program to your precise specifications. A donor-advised fund is less expensive to establish initially and on an ongoing basis than a private foundation.

Additional advantages include seclusion and tranquility. In contrast to an IRS private foundation, a family foundation that operates via a donor-advised fund is not obliged to submit detailed financial information such as tax returns. Aside from that, the stringent and complicated legal requirements of a private foundation vanish—no more concerns about compensation restrictions, costs, grant spending obligations, tax filings, or accidental self-dealing.

Despite the fact that private foundations are effective vehicles for charitable giving, they may not be the best match for your objectives. Discover why donor-advised funds may be a more convenient option.

Raising Funds

It may take several months or even years to get your permanent tax-exempt status after submitting your application, but you should receive a letter within a few months verifying that your first application seems to be valid and permitting you to begin fund-raising activities. You should be aware that if the exemption is canceled in the future, you will lose this status. After receiving the preliminary letter, you may realistically expect to be recognized as tax-exempt and begin fundraising, barring unforeseen circumstances.

Fundraising and the politics of the nonprofit sector are too vast for this book, but it should be mentioned that several books and hired consultants explain how to accomplish it. It is never simple, and far too many foundations devote a disproportionate amount of time to fundraising rather than doing important work. You should carefully evaluate your budget's revenue sources and the inevitable delay in collecting money.

If all or a substantial part of your finances will come from you or your family, you may encounter extra obstacles in gaining tax-exempt status or deductions. You should contact a skilled accountant and attorney before incorporating any strategy.

This is especially true if your family will get a substantial share of the foundation's income. The government does not want your family to profit from a tax-free structure if they do not actively engage in tax-exempt activities. It is possible to pay a wage, but it is safer to have contributions from other sources and to make payments to non-family members.

Conclusion

A foundation is a charitable trust or non-profit organization that awards grants to other philanthropic organizations. In contrast, a foundation may directly participate in charitable operations. Contributors to charitable foundations may adopt a strategic philanthropic giving strategy (donors can be families, individuals, organizations, etc.).

<u>FAQs:</u>

Is there a minimum amount of money a private foundation must distribute?

When the United States government provides tax-exempt status to a private foundation, it expects the foundation to spend its income to benefit society. The government mandates that the foundation donate at least a portion of its annual assets to charitable groups. The name of this regulation is the payment obligation.

This sum is paid by foundations via qualified distributions, the majority of which are grants. In certain instances, administrative costs associated with giving grants may be eligible. To avoid paying taxes, a private foundation must typically meet or exceed an annual contribution threshold of 5% of the average market value of its net investment assets.

If you are a charity in need of finances, you may benefit from the payment requirement. If you know how much a private foundation has in assets, you may estimate how much it must pay out in grants each year to satisfy its payment obligation

The Foundation Data Office (FDO) maintains accurate data on more than 150,000 private foundations, including foundation assets. You may pay for FDO or use it for free on the websites of the Funding Information Network.

You may also review Form 990-PF to learn about a private foundation's assets and grants

Do all private foundations qualify as tax-exempt?

The Internal Revenue Service classifies both private foundations and public charities as 501(c)(3) entities. Each has positive societal benefits. Private foundations and public charities, on the other hand, have distinct methods for achieving and sustaining their purposes, as well as for self-government. In other words, yes.

How Much Money Is Necessary to Establish a Private Foundation?

Private foundations are often supported by a single person, family, or company. They may use a range of assets to support themselves and retain them. After receiving contributions, other forms of donating vehicles often liquidate non-publicly traded assets.

A private foundation may own the assets listed below:

- Cash and government bonds
- Alternative investments, including private equity
- Real estate investing
- Physical property (art, jewelry, collectibles)
- Intellectual property (copyrights, patents, royalties)
- Retirement and life insurance

If you have a Charitable Remainder Trust, your nonprofit organization may be the beneficiary. Managers collaborate closely with the reputable financial adviser you choose, providing their knowledge of the unique conditions that influence the assets of a private foundation.

Private foundations have considerable discretion in pursuing their philanthropic objectives. In addition to assisting public charities and other sorts of organizations, a foundation may also:

- Provide funding for catastrophe relief and economic suffering.
- Make loans in exchange for compensation to the foundation.
- Create reward and scholarship programs and choose beneficiaries.
- Provide assistance to international organizations.
- Donate to for-profit organizations so long as the revenues are used for a philanthropic cause.
- Develop its own philanthropic activities, such as a coat drive or soup kitchen.

Should we form our foundation as a trust or a company?

When the legal owner of assets transfers legal ownership to people or a company for the benefit of family and friends, a trust is created. On the other hand, foundations are seen as a mix between a trust and a corporation. A foundation is a non-stock corporation controlled in line with its rules by a council. A foundation must be registered in order to exist, but a trust is an arrangement between two parties that does not need registration.

There is also a distinction between the owner of the assets that a trustee manages on behalf of a trust and the trustee. In contrast, foundations do not impose such divisions since they hold all of their assets entirely. The two most prevalent forms of charity trusts are charitable lead and charitable remainder trusts. A trust is established when assets are deposited in it and the annual income is contributed to charity. The structure has been drastically altered. In a charitable residual trust, beneficiaries and donors are compensated before the charity.

This ensures that the recipients will get a steady income. There are a variety of foundation types, each with its unique qualities. Because there are so many charitable foundations, it may be difficult to evaluate them. To classify them, you must examine the many jobs they do and their supporting components. In contrast, foundations may be split into different categories:

- Volunteering for a charitable organization
- The institution of the neighborhood
- Endowment funds for corporations
- A charitable organization
- Organizations providing financial support
- Structural support for a cultural institution

What function do charity trusts serve?

You may put your assets to work for you, your beneficiaries, and charitable organizations via a charitable trust. A trust may provide benevolent individuals with non-essential assets such as real estate or stocks with a range of financial benefits. A trust is a legal entity that enables an individual to transfer assets or gifts to a charity.

What are the costs of starting a non-profit?

The cost of incorporation might vary from $8 to $1,098 depending on where you live. In quite a few states, registration as a charity is necessary and may incur extra costs. The average cost to register a name, with a range of $0 to $425, is $85.91.

Registration as a Business:

In some states, you will need a business license, but this charge may be waived in certain areas, while others may not require further company registration.

The average cost of establishing a company is $170.38. At $412.50, the District of Columbia had the highest price.

State-Specific Fees:

These are fees that are specific to each state and are necessary for certain circumstances. For example, sales tax and other payments could add up to $194.63.

Your results may vary based on the nature and complexity of your business. Reputable businesses, charge between $1,699 and $2,549 for quality work. We advise avoiding the $149 packages, which are prohibitively expensive.

Should you hire a lawyer? Using a competent, seasoned attorney to incorporate a nonprofit company is unquestionably the most advantageous course of action. However, this may be a more expensive choice. The hourly rate of an attorney normally ranges from $150 to $500.

When you consider that participating in a charitable endeavor may take 16 hours or more, you might expect to spend between $2,400 and $8,000. Some attorneys provide flat-rate packages for the formation of nonprofit organizations. Others may charge nonprofit organizations a lower cost. A significant amount of money may be saved by preparing all of the paperwork yourself.

Get volunteers:

 Do you have a personal network or are you acquainted with a local lawyer? You may always enquire about their services to see whether they are willing to do the task for free. Consult with other nongovernmental groups to seek advice.

What other expenses are there? In addition to state and federal filing fees, incorporating a nonprofit company incurs extra expenses. Other considerations include liability insurance, which is among the various forms of coverage.

Locate a merchant:

Rent an office, supplies, and other office equipment. Will you need telephone and Internet service? It is not recommended to use your own phone number. Examples of brands include logos, signs, and marketing collateral. This costs money as well. Non-profits should have their own bank accounts. Combining personal and corporate finances is not advisable.

Hire an accountant:

You will probably want the counsel, if not the aid, of a CPA with knowledge of nonprofit finances and tax laws.

Conclusion:

State and federal fees may total $2,448 when establishing a nonprofit organization. If you need help from an attorney, it might cost up to $10,248 but could be as little as $283 if you get pro bono assistance.

What options are there for managing a private foundation?

Operating your own foundation may be hard, time-consuming, and subject you to costly compliance errors while being cost-effective.

Putting together a team of specialists you know and trust (a lawyer, a financial adviser, an accountant, etc.) seems perfect, and if they already manage your other business, it may be cost-efficient. In contrast, coordinating their operations requires time and effort, and they may lack foundation-specific knowledge, leading to errors.

Frequently, trust departments provide foundation administration services, but you must maintain the foundation's assets at their institution, employ their managers, and abide by their regulations. Despite the fact that their administrative services seem to be "free," the cost is sometimes concealed in investment management and other fees.

<u>References:</u>

EA, Greg McRay. "Before You Start: Define Your Nonprofit Purpose - Foundation Group®." *Foundation Group®*, www.501c3.org, 13 Sept. 2016, https://www.501c3.org/before-you-start-define-your-nonprofit-purpose-programs/.

"How to Start a Private Foundation: 10 Steps (with Pictures)." *wikiHow*, www.wikihow.com, 17 Mar. 2022, https://www.wikihow.com/Start-a-Private-Foundation.

"Factors to Consider When Creating Your Foundation: Corporation or Trust? | Our Insights | Plante Moran." *Factors to Consider When Creating Your Foundation: Corporation or Trust? | Our Insights | Plante Moran*, www.plantemoran.com, 19 July 2021, https://www.plantemoran.com/explore-our-thinking/insight/2021/07/factors-to-consider-when-beginning-your-foundation-corporation-or-trust.

"Trustee Compensation: Should Your Foundation Pay? | GMA Foundations." *GMA*

Foundations, www.gmafoundations.com, 20 July 2017, https://www.gmafoundations.com/trustee-compensation-private-foundation/.

"Setting Up Your Own Foundation: The Basic Law Procedure | Stimmel Law." *Setting Up Your Own Foundation: The Basic Law Procedure | Stimmel Law*, www.stimmel-law.com, https://www.stimmel-law.com/en/articles/setting-your-own-foundation-basic-law-procedure. Accessed 28 May 2022.

"What Is a Foundation? Definitions, Types & Rules | Foundation Source." *Foundation Source*, foundationsource.com, 11 Mar. 2022, https://foundationsource.com/learn-about-foundations/what-is-a-private-foundation/#:~:text=Private%20foundations%20and%20public%20charities,as%20well%20as%20governing%20themselves.

"Candid Learning | Trainings in Nonprofit Fundraising, Proposal Writing, Grants." *Candid Learning*, learning.candid.org, https://learning.candid.org/resources/knowledge-

base/payout/#:~:text=Generally%2C%20a%20p
rivate%20foundation%20must,assets%20to%2
0avoid%20paying%20taxes. Accessed 28 May
2022.

"Starting a Private Foundation | Hurwit &
Associates." *Hurwit & Associates*,
www.hurwitassociates.com, 6 Oct. 2021,
https://www.hurwitassociates.com/starting-
up-nonprofit-foundation-basics/starting-a-
foundation-advantages-and-disadvantages/.

"How to Start & Set Up a Foundation |
Foundation Source." *Foundation Source*,
foundationsource.com, 11 Mar. 2022,
https://foundationsource.com/start-a-
foundation/.

"Private Foundations vs. Public Charities."
Investopedia, www.investopedia.com, 18 Mar.
2022,
https://www.investopedia.com/financial-
edge/1112/the-difference-between-private-
foundations-and-public-charities.aspx.

"Employer Identification Number | Internal
Revenue Service." *Employer Identification
Number | Internal Revenue Service*,
www.irs.gov, https://www.irs.gov/charities-

non-profits/employer-identification-
number#:~:text=To%20apply%20for%20an%20
employer,the%20U.S.%20or%20U.S.%20territo
ries. Accessed 28 May 2022.

"Top 10 Advantages of Having a Private
Foundation." *Top 10 Advantages of Having a
Private Foundation*, www.oppenheimer.com, 3
Dec. 2020,
https://www.oppenheimer.com/perkinsgroup/
2020/insight/december/top-10-advantages-of-
having-a-private-foundation-print.aspx.

"The Pros and Cons of Being a Nonprofit."
Investopedia, www.investopedia.com, 26 May
2022,
https://www.investopedia.com/articles/investi
ng/110215/pros-and-cons-being-nonprofit.asp.

Kim, Jiah. "Charitable Trust vs. Foundation: Key
Differences - A Comprehensive Guide - Jiah Kim
& Associates." *Jiah Kim & Associates*,
jiahkimlaw.com, 13 Apr. 2022,
https://jiahkimlaw.com/estate-
planning/charitable-trust-vs-foundation-key-
differences/.

"Options for Managing a Private Foundation -
Foundation Source." *Foundation Source*,

foundationsource.com, 20 Apr. 2021,
https://foundationsource.com/resources/hub/
resource/options-for-managing-a-private-
foundation-2/.